MW00936203

School For Wisdom Apostolic Lessons

Apostle G. Marie Carroll

School For Wisdom
Apostolic Lessons

For more information about Apostle G. Marie Carroll
Contact:
516 833-5235
Or kingdombuilders669@yahoo.com
Cover Design: Blaze
Editing: Apostle G. Marie Carroll/Blaze

Printed in the United States of America

Dedication

I dedicate this book to anyone who chooses to receive this dedication and make it their own! God has given you a multitude of seeds and in those seeds there are seeds.

Be Fruitful and Multiply!

Table of Contents

Introduction

There are times when the Lord will minister to me about various subjects that will help in the equipping of the saints. I have compiled five teachings of empowerment and included some prophetic application and questions that will challenge every believer.

Those who are looking to go deeper in their understanding of God and His purpose for us will be stirred in revelation and powered to move into another dimension of God's Glory! I thank God for this Seed!

Grace and Peace,

Apostle G. Marie Carroll

Lesson 1:

Seed, Time, Harvest

Genesis 1:11-12 "And God said, Let the earth bring forth grass, the herb yielding seed, and the fruit tree yielding fruit after his kind, whose seed is in itself, upon the earth: and it was so. And the earth brought forth grass, and herb yielding seed after his kind, and the tree yielding fruit, whose seed was in itself, after his kind: and God saw that it was good." Genesis 1:29 And God said, Behold, I have given you every herb bearing seed, which is upon the face of all the earth, and every tree, in the which is the fruit of a tree yielding seed; to you it shall be for meat."

Genesis 8:22 "While the earth remaineth, seedtime and harvest, and cold and heat, and summer and winter, and day and night shall not cease."

.

John 12:24 "Verily, verily, I say unto you, Except a corn of wheat fall into the ground and die, it abideth alone: but if it die, it bringeth forth much fruit. 1 Corinthians 15:36 Thou fool, that which thou sowest is not quickened, except it die:"

Ecclesiastes 11:4 "He that observeth the wind shall not sow; and he that regardeth the clouds shall not reap."

Ecclesiastes 11:6 "In the morning sow thy seed, and in the evening withhold not thine hand: for thou knowest not whether shall prosper, either this or that, or whether they both shall be alike good."

Timothy was a young farmer in North Carolina who inherited a farm from his father. For years Timothy's father Daniel had spoken with him about learning the tricks of the trade but Tim was not interested.   After many years of speaking with Timothy (to no avail) Daniel died and left the farm to Timothy as an inheritance.

Young Timothy knew nothing about seed time or harvest and after one year the land became barren. For some reason Timothy thought that the land would just keep producing even though he had planted nothing. So Timothy still not willing to learn or ask how to be a real farmer planted some corn seed. A short time after He planted the seed he did not see anything come up so He dug up the seed and replanted it in another part of the field and waited for a short time and when he did not see anything come up he did the same thing again. Then he did not see anything after a short time and he gave up and walked away from the field.

He eventually sold the property to the neighboring farmer and that farmer understanding the laws of Seed, Time, and Harvest plowed the land, prepared the ground, sowed ample seed and waited for the time of Harvest. That man reaped a mighty harvest because he took the time to know the principles that God himself set into motion when He created Heaven and Earth.

It is important that we know the principles of God if we want to reap the benefits of God. It is all about the SEED, The Time of Waiting and then the Season of Harvest!!

The Bible tells us in **2 Corinthians 9:6** If we want to reap sparingly (stingily) then sow sparingly, BUT If we want to reap Bountifully (Pressed down shaken together and running OVER) then we must SOW Bountifully. God is so good that He will leave the choice up to us. Big Blessings require Big Sowing. Even farmers know if they want a great harvest they have to sow ample SEED!

Genesis 1:11-12 "And God said, Let the earth bring forth grass, the herb yielding seed, and the fruit tree yielding fruit after his kind, whose seed is in itself, upon the earth: and it was so. And the earth brought forth grass and herb yielding seed after his kind, and the tree yielding fruit, whose seed was in itself, after his kind: and God saw that it was good."

Father's words spoken were seeds sown that yielded a product. ... "Whose seed is in itself" means that everything that the Lord made has the ability to reproduce after it own kind because the seed of that thing is already on the inside when it was created.

Think about a human baby, it is already equipped with reproductive organs to produce another human being, given the right circumstances. God's word will not go out and come back lacking, it shall produce what He intended! God saw... means He was watching over His seed and knew that It was Good.

Genesis 1:29 "And God said, Behold, I have given you every herb bearing seed, which is upon the face of all the earth, and every tree, in the which is the fruit of a tree yielding seed; to you it shall be for meat."

From the beginning of time the Lord has used the concept of seeds to reveal Himself to us. In every way we must recognize that our seed whether it is our children, our ministry, our money, our mission, our relationships and even our food if planted correctly will produce tremendous fruit. Our Father knows what we need and if we follow His orders completely we will yield the return that was promised to us before the foundation of the world**. (Romans 8:29)**

Each kind of seed has its own body.

1 Corinthians 15:38 "But God giveth it a body as it hath pleased him, and to every seed his own body."

We are considered seeds, just as Christ was a seed planted (buried) and resurrected that He may be the firstborn of many men **(Romans 8:29).**

It is imperative that we understand the concept of seeds if we are to receive the full revelation of the Kingdom. The Kingdom message is based on Seed, Time and Harvest. We must sow (seed) to the Spirit if we want to reap Life eternal with God. If we sow (seed or feed) our flesh (worldly view) we will reap corruption which is separation from our Father eternally.

Sowing of Seed
Time for sowing is called seed-time.

Genesis 8:22 "While the earth remaineth, seedtime and harvest, and cold and heat, and summer and winter, and day and night shall not cease."

This is a covenant made by God to Noah, that He would never destroy all flesh again and that as long as there is an earth there will be seedtime and Harvest…

For this study we want to continue to look at Seed, for as long as there is an earth there will be seeds to plant, a time to wait and a period to go into the harvest.

Necessary to its productivity:

John 12:24 "Verily, verily, I say unto you, Except a corn of wheat fall into the ground and die, it abideth alone: but if it die, it bringeth forth much fruit."

Jesus was ministering to the disciples about his impending death and resurrection. At this time the disciples had no idea what was really being said but His words have been recorded that we might benefit and know that we are recipients of the resurrection because Jesus committed Himself to obedience and the fruit thereof.

Each kind of seed has its own body.

1 Corinthians 15:36 "Thou fool, that which thou sowest is not quickened, except it die:"

A seed must die, carnality must die, and lustfulness must die if we expect to have a godly harvest. In this passage Paul is speaking to the Corinthians about the last day when the dead in Christ shall rise. How the trumpet shall sound. He is using the simplest form to parallel the resurrection and that is how God created the trees and herbs, and man from a seed with a seed already in them and how once that seed produces fruit it can continue to produce fruit forever. The same with the resurrection, once Christ was planted His resurrection caused trillions of souls who now believe to have seeds in them to plant in others.

Required: Constant diligence.

Ecclesiastes 11:4 "He that observeth the wind shall not sow; and he that regardeth the clouds shall not reap."

Ecclesiastes 11:6 "In the morning sow thy seed, and in the evening withhold not thine hand: for thou knowest not whether shall prosper, either this or that, or whether they both shall be alike good."

Father is looking for those who are willing to wait on their harvest and not dig up the plant before it has roots. Trust is necessary for the germination of our Seed. Trust is parallel to Time. When we trust God we will give Him time to do a work in us that is excellent and marvelous in his eyes. When we give Him time to mold and shape us we show Him that we trust Him.

Timothy, the farmer in our story did not have this information. He is a reminder to us that we must trust God! If we look at our situations we will not trust God to sow and when we look at our situation we will not trust Him to gather either. We are at a standstill when we have no trust in what our Father has already shown us through His word and even in our own testimony.

So, what God has already given us we Sow it, we do not close our hands up in any situation because we may be closing our hands up on our own prosperity. In the morning Sow and continue to be a Sower and watch the Lord move mightily! God Gives seed to the Sower!

Required to be watered by the rain.

Isaiah 55:10-11 "For as the rain cometh down, and the snow from heaven, and returneth not thither, but watereth the earth, and maketh it bring forth and bud, that it may give seed to the sower, and bread to the eater:
so is my word that goes out from my mouth: It will not return to me empty, but will accomplish what I desire and achieve the purpose for which I sent it." (NIV)

There is a guarantee that no matter what the Lord's purpose for our lives will be accomplished. It is up to us to continue to sow the seeds that He has given to us. The gifts, the money, the time that He has given must be sown back in order to reap a great harvest. In **Isaiah 55:10** the Bible says just as God gives elements to water the earth these elements are seeds as well that causes the earth to bud and the buds have seeds which cause reapers to have seed that they can now take to sow into others that seeds would continue to be produced eternally.

Father has sent His word. His word is full of seeds and all it takes is for his children to catch this revelation and begin to sow no matter what may come or go.

Sow and Trust God, Sow and be a witness to His power, Sow and serve, Sow and wait on the manifestation of the Glory. He sent His word to heal, deliver, and set the captives free and to bring prosperity into the lives of those who have lack. We just need to Sow into the word and expect a great Harvest in the fullness of Time!

Food For Thought:

1) If Christ should arrive here in the next 5 minutes, what have you sown (in your time here on Earth) to the Kingdom of God that has yielded a Harvest?

2) No man knows the day nor the hour when the Son of Man shall come, are you ready to trust God and Sow the seeds He trusted you with? Time, Talent, Treasure?

Harvest = the season when ripened crops are gathered.

Reap = to gather or take (a crop, harvest, etc.) to cut (wheat, rye, etc.) with a sickle or other implement or a machine, as in harvest.

Can you see the difference between these two words?

The Tithe/The Offering

(The tenth of all your substance/As the Lord Prospers You)
Malachi 3:8-10 "Will a man rob God? Yet you rob me. But you ask, 'How do we rob you?' In tithes and offerings. You are under a curse—the whole nation of you—because you are robbing me. Bring the whole tithe into the storehouse, that there may be food in my house. Test me in this," says the LORD Almighty, "and see if I will not throw open the floodgates of heaven and pour out so much blessing that you will not have room enough for it." (NIV)

Is there anything wrong with this scripture?
Why do we suppose people are not willing to comply with God's Word?

2 Corinthians 9:6-11" Remember this: Whoever sows sparingly will also reap sparingly, and whoever sows generously will also reap generously. Each man should give what he has decided in his heart to give, not

reluctantly or under compulsion, for God loves a cheerful giver. And God is able to make all grace abound to you, so that in all things at all times, having all that you need, you will abound in every good work. As it is written: 'He has scattered abroad his gifts to the poor; his righteousness endures forever.' Now he who supplies seed to the sower and bread for food will also supply and increase your store of seed and will enlarge the harvest of your righteousness. You will be made rich in every way so that you can be generous on every occasion, and through us your generosity will result in thanksgiving to God." (NIV)

New Testament Tithes are for those who want to stretch their faith to enlarge their territory!

The Prophetic Application

Apply the following principles to an everyday situation.

God wants to increase you in your finances what must you do?

God wants to stir up ministry in you what must you do?

God is seeking someone to head up a project at the church and you have the skills what must you do?

There is a need in the ministry and you have the Treasure, the Time or the Talent what must you do?

God has entrusted you with Gifts to profit a certain church, where must you be?

God has given you a talent that can impact the world how will you proceed?

Prophesy to someone in your area.

Questions

1. What was the main characters problem?

2. What was missing from the equation?

3. What scripture would you have used to encourage the Main Character?

4. How will you now use this information to better serve Christ?

5. Does God give_____ to the _____?

How? Give examples

6. What was created with a seed already inside of it?

7. What will God Complete in you?

Share Your Lesson with family, friends and neighbors and the Lord will bless you for sowing seeds for the Kingdom!

Lesson 2:

A Good Soil

Matthew 13:2-10, 18-23 "And he spake many things unto them in parables, saying, Behold, a sower went forth to sow; And when he sowed, some seeds fell by the way side, and the fowls came and devoured them up: Some fell upon stony places, where they had not much earth: and forthwith they sprung up, because they had no deepness of earth: And when the sun was up, they were scorched; and because they had no root, they withered away. And some fell among thorns; and the thorns sprung up, and choked them: But other fell into good ground, and brought forth fruit, some an hundredfold, some sixtyfold, some thirtyfold. Who hath ears to hear, let him hear. And the disciples came, and said unto him, Why speakest thou unto them in parables?"

"Hear ye therefore the parable of the sower. When any one heareth the word of the kingdom, and understandeth it not, then cometh the wicked one, and catcheth away that which was sown in his heart. This is he which received seed by the way side. But he that received the seed into stony places, the same is he that heareth the word, and anon with joy receiveth it; Yet hath he not root in himself, but dureth for a while: for when tribulation or persecution ariseth because of the word, by and by he is offended. He also that received seed among the thorns is he that heareth the word; and the care of this world, and the deceitfulness of riches, choke the word, and he becometh unfruitful. But he that received seed into the good ground is he that heareth the word, and understandeth it; which also beareth fruit, and bringeth forth, some an hundredfold, some sixty, some thirty."

Emily loved the praise and worship at the church and was so happy when the praise team would sing her favorite song. She would sing and clap and love the Lord while at the church and all was well as long as she was at the church. When the word went forth it was so exciting to her but much of it she did not understand because most of her life she only opened her Bible at the church and even then she wasn't really reading it. It was the music that was really giving her joy.

Emily had a powerful job as a director of health care at a major company and life was really good. She owned a great car, a nice home and she even had a great husband and children but she was still searching for something that seemed to be missing.

Not too long after Emily's salvation she lost her job and the families finances became so strained that their home went into foreclosure.

At first Emily kept on coming to church and singing along with the praise and worship team but after a few weeks the joy that she had began to dwindle away and she started looking at her situation and depression seeped in. The more the Pastor preached on Sowing the more offended Emily became. Emily kept saying "How can I give what I don't have?" She did not realize that the Lord wanted her to give herself to Him in studying, in time, and in talent.

Her offence continued until she found herself out of the presence of the Lord. Emily was blessed to belong to a church that watches and cares for the flock. The Pastor called her and ministered to her about the parable of the sower. He was able to show Emily her life and she realized the terrible condition of her heart (soil).

Emily repented, joined the bible study group and not long after became a powerful teacher of the Gospel of Jesus Christ ministering all over the world.

Matthew 13:19-22 "When any one heareth the word of the kingdom, and understandeth it not, then cometh the wicked one, and catcheth away that which was sown in his heart. This is he which received seed by the way side."

We must be careful that we are not the one that attends church but fail to understand the sermon. This walk is personal and our relationship with God is the principle thing. If we are not aware of His word then we have no idea what his promises are. The enemy loves this, now he can talk and cause us to believe him since we will not take the time to get to know our Father through His word.

"But he that received the seed into stony places, the same is he that heareth the word, and anon with joy receiveth it; Yet hath he not root in himself, but dureth for a while: for when tribulation or persecution ariseth because of the word, by and by he is offended."

This reminds me of the baby Christian. They are those who go with how they feel **Today!**

It is not about feelings, it is about what we are chosen to do and feelings have nothing to do with it. As soon as they are chastised by the word the one who has received on stony ground gets offended and is ready to leave the church, forget about their ministry, and forget all about what God told them to do. There is no root that will cause them to stand like the trees by the rivers of water that shall not be moved.

"He also that received seed among the thorns is he that heareth the word; and the care of this world, and the deceitfulness of riches, choke the word, and he becometh unfruitful."

This is our carnal Christian, wonderful, giving and most of the time an all around nice person until it is time to put God before their family, cars, houses and jobs.

This Christian reminds me of the rich ruler in **Luke 18:18-25** "And a certain ruler asked him, saying, Good Master, what shall I do to inherit eternal life? And Jesus said unto him, Why callest thou me good? none is good, save one, that is, God. Thou knowest the commandments, Do not commit adultery, Do not kill, Do not steal, Do not bear false witness, Honour thy father and thy mother. And he said, All these have I kept from my youth up. Now when Jesus heard these things, he said unto him, Yet lackest thou one thing: sell all that thou hast, and distribute unto the poor, and thou shalt have treasure in heaven: and come, follow me. And when he heard this, he was very sorrowful: for he was very rich. And when Jesus saw that he was very sorrowful, he said, How hardly shall they that have riches enter into the kingdom of God! For it is easier for a camel to go through a needle's eye, than for a rich man to enter into the kingdom of God.

This ruler represents a Christian with seeds sown on thorny ground, the word has been choked and his riches have deceived him. His choices have caused him to lose eternal life with Christ Jesus.

"But he that received seed into the good ground is he that heareth the word, and understandeth it; which also beareth fruit, and bringeth forth, some an hundredfold, some sixty, some thirty."

This Christian is a follower of Jesus Christ, a hearer and a doer of the Word of God. We shall know them by their fruit.

The word of the Lord speaks volumes on those who are called of God and the fruit which remains if the ones who are chosen abide in the vine.

John 15:1-9 "I am the true vine, and my Father is the husbandman. Every branch in me that beareth not fruit he taketh away: and every branch that beareth fruit, he purgeth it, that it may bring forth more fruit. Now ye are clean through the word which I have spoken unto you. Abide in me, and I in you. As the branch cannot bear fruit of itself, except it abide in the vine; no more can ye, except ye abide in me. I am the vine, ye are the branches: He that abideth in me, and I in him, the same bringeth forth much fruit: for without me ye can do nothing. If a man abideth not in me, he is cast forth as a branch, and is withered; and men gather them, and cast them into the fire, and they are burned. If ye abide in me, and my words abide in you, ye shall ask what ye will, and it shall be done unto you.Herein is my Father glorified, that ye bear much fruit; so shall ye be my disciples. As the Father hath loved me, so have I loved you: continue ye in my love."

      This is the Christian who has decided to make Jesus their choice. This person knows the difference between the Form of godliness and the TRUE WORSHIPPER!

Food for Thought

1) If Christ were to come in the next five minutes what condition would He find your heart in? Please be honest with your self, true deliverance can come only through honesty.

2) No man knows the day nor the hour when the Son of Man shall come, are you ready to trust God and allow Him to prepare your heart for seeds that will produce fruit that will remain?

SOIL=any place or condition providing the opportunity for growth or development:

GROUND=the solid surface of the earth; firm or dry land.

Can you see the difference between these two words?

The Tithe/The Offering

(The tenth of all your substance/As the Lord Prospers You)
Malachi 3:8-10 "Will a man rob God? Yet you rob me. But you ask, 'How do we rob you?' In tithes and offerings. You are under a curse—the whole nation of you—because you are robbing me. Bring the whole tithe into the storehouse, that there may be food in my house. Test me in this," says the LORD Almighty, "and see if I will not throw open the floodgates of heaven and pour out so much blessing that you will not have room enough for it." (NIV)

Is there anything wrong with this scripture?
Why do we suppose people are not willing to comply with God's Word?

2 Corinthians 9:6-11" Remember this: Whoever sows sparingly will also reap sparingly, and whoever sows generously will also reap generously.

Each man should give what he has decided in his heart to give, not reluctantly or under compulsion, for God loves a cheerful giver. And God is able to make all grace abound to you, so that in all things at all times, having all that you need, you will abound in every good work. As it is written: 'He has scattered abroad his gifts to the poor; his righteousness endures forever.' Now he who supplies seed to the sower and bread for food will also supply and increase your store of seed and will enlarge the harvest of your righteousness. You will be made rich in every way so that you can be generous on every occasion, and through us your generosity will result in thanksgiving to God." (NIV)

New Testament Tithes are for those who want to stretch their faith to enlarge their territory!

The Prophetic Application

Apply the following principles to an everyday situation.

1) You are in the church and you cannot understand the word that is going forth, what will you do?

a. Act like you know
b. Take notes and ask the pastor or another leader after church
c. Ask your friend who is not a Christian
d. Not care you will catch it next week

2) Pastor has preached a great word and you get home and there are situations you don't care for what will you do?

a. Go to the phone and tell everybody what happened
b. Call the Pastor and ask for godly counsel
c. Give all of them a piece of your mind, expletives and all

d. Devise a plan to get them back later

3) You have received a prophetic word about your finances and instead of things getting better they seem to be getting worse what will you do?

a. Take matters in your own hands and do creative financing
b. Call up some old friends who know the streets and get the job done
c. Get a job working on Sunday I really don't need church anyway
d. Trust in God and Wait for Him to move according to His Word

Prophesy to someone in your area and encourage them on preparing their ground!

Questions

1. What was the main characters problem?

2. What was missing from the equation?

3. What scripture would you have used to encourage the main character   ?

4. How will you now use this information to better serve Christ?

5. It is easier for a_____ to go through the _____, than for a_____

Why? Give examples

6. What kind of ground does the Lord Love?

Why?

Share Your Lesson with family, friends and neighbors and the Lord will bless you for sowing seeds for the Kingdom!

Lesson 3:

The Talents

Matthew 25:14-30 "For the kingdom of heaven is as a man travelling into a far country, who called his own servants, and delivered unto them his goods. And unto one he gave five talents, to another two, and to another one; to every man according to his several ability; and straightway took his journey. Then he that had received the five talents went and traded with the same, and made them other five talents. And likewise he that had received two, he also gained other two. But he that had received one went and digged in the earth, and hid his lord's money. After a long time the lord of those servants cometh, and reckoneth with them. And so he that had received five talents came and brought other five talents, saying, Lord, thou deliveredst unto me five talents: behold,

I have gained beside them five talents more. His lord said unto him, Well done, thou good and faithful servant: thou hast been faithful over a few things, I will make thee ruler over many things: enter thou into the joy of thy lord. He also that had received two talents came and said, Lord, thou deliveredst unto me two talents: behold, I have gained two other talents beside them. His lord said unto him, Well done, good and faithful servant; thou hast been faithful over a few things, I will make thee ruler over many things: enter thou into the joy of thy lord. Then he which had received the one talent came and said, Lord, I knew thee that thou art an hard man, reaping where thou hast not sown, and gathering where thou hast not strawed: And I was afraid, and went and hid thy talent in the earth: lo, there thou hast that is thine. His lord answered and said unto him, Thou wicked and slothful servant, thou knewest that I reap where I sowed not, and gather where I have not strawed: Thou oughtest therefore to have put my money to the exchangers, and then at my coming I should have

received mine own with usury. Take therefore the talent from him, and give it unto him which hath ten talents.
For unto every one that hath shall be given, and he shall have abundance: but from him that hath not shall be taken away even that which he hath. And cast ye the unprofitable servant into outer darkness: there shall be weeping and gnashing of teeth."

Patty and Andy Brown owned a Christian Bookstore in their neighborhood. After much hard work and prayer their business began to flourish. Soon after an opportunity to increase their business was presented to them by the local church where they were members.

The idea was a new design for Choir Robes for the youth and required a minimal investment and this would draw business from the other churches. Patty and Andy had fears of failure so they would not hear of any ideas to increase what they already had. Andy was so fearful that He did not use the banks and interest could not be made on any of their profits.

Competition moved into the area and their business slowly dwindled. Their church was forced to use the new business to get their idea across and now the idea is used by many of the churches around the world. The window of opportunity closed and Andy and Patty lost their business.

Matthew 25:14-30 "For the kingdom of heaven is as a man travelling into a far country, who called his own servants, and delivered unto them his goods.
This scripture is telling us that the gifts that are inside of us and all that we own belongs to God, he just loaned them to us to steward.(advance the Kingdom)

And unto one he gave five talents, to another two, and to another one; to every man according to his several

ability; and straightway took his journey.
To each of us he has given something, some more than others according to what He knows we can handle.

Then he that had received the five talents went and traded with the same, and made them other five talents.

Some Christians trust God so much that no matter what they will try to increase whatever He has given to them. That is why we find those like Israel Houghton, every time he hears from God musically; He ends up making a CD for others to hear from God. He is a good steward over the talent that God has given him.

And likewise he that had received two, he also gained other two."

Now we have some who are not as famous as Israel but are still in the studios all over the country recording and people on their computers blogging and some on their laptops writing books, and are stewarding whatever they have no matter how small.

"But he that had received one went and digged in the earth, and hid his lord's money. "

And we have some who are not willing to try because they feel that what they have is not enough and they are not willing to risk what they have to get more.

I have had experience with those who God has given musical ability, degrees in education, books, CD's, photography,artists, play instruments, handle finances and administrate churches and yet they will hide that talent and refuse to sow into the work of God.

"After a long time the lord of those servants cometh, and reckoneth with them."

The Bible says a day of accountability shall come and everyone will have to give an account of all the gifts that God gave to them to use to advance His Kingdom.

"And so he that had received five talents came and brought other five talents, saying, Lord, thou deliveredst unto me five talents: behold, I have gained beside them five talents more.
This Child of God did what the Lord would calls the greater work, he doubled what the Lord gave him

His lord said unto him, Well done, thou good and faithful servant: thou hast been faithful over a few things, I will make thee ruler over many things: enter thou into the joy of thy lord.

Now his territory has been enlarged and because of his faithfulness he has become a ruler and rulers administrate, they are not the laborer.

He also that had received two talents came and said, Lord, thou deliveredst unto me two talents: behold, I have gained two other talents beside them."

Same as the above... Father what little you gave me I used it for Your glory. You told me to usher I did it to the best of my ability. There was no job too big or too small. He doubled what he had.

"His lord said unto him, Well done, good and faithful servant; thou hast been faithful over a few things, I will make thee ruler over many things: enter thou into the joy of thy lord."

Well done child of God, now you shall rule and reign as well and rulers do not serve, they are served. Enter into the joy of the Lord.

"Then he which had received the one talent came and said, Lord, I knew thee that thou art an hard man,

reaping where thou hast not sown, and gathering where thou hast not strawed:"

Gave an excuse for not using the talent, blamed everything on the master, presumptuous, heady and slothful.

"And I was afraid, and went and hid thy talent in the earth: lo, there thou hast that is thine."

He gave Father back the same thing God gave him. He never even tried to fulfill the will of the Lord in his life.

I am reminded of a friend of mine who has decided that she is a Buddhist and no matter what I say she is determined that this is her faith. Well in the meantime the Lord has called her to be an Evangelist in His church but she is busy hiding in another religion. When Jesus comes he will be looking for the gifts He gave her to be increased and she will not have them ready unless repentance is granted to her.

**"His lord answered and said unto
him, Thou wicked and slothful
servant, thou knewest that I reap
where I sowed not, and gather where
I have not strawed:**

He was judged because of his choices
to be lazy!

**Thou oughtest therefore to have put
my money to the exchangers, and
then at my coming I should have
received mine own with usury."**

God wants us to use what He has
given us. God wants us to try Him and
watch Him bless us exceedingly and
abundantly!

**"Take therefore the talent from him,
and give it unto him which hath ten
talents.**

Oh my God, what we will not use He will
take and give to someone who is not
afraid to believe the word and go forth in
Boldness and invest in their gift.

"For unto every one that hath shall be given, and he shall have abundance: but from him that hath not shall be taken away even that which he hath."

The one that has an ear to hear God and enough courage to believe God will be increased, the one that hath not an ear to hear and is fearful will lose what little he does know about the Kingdom of God.

"And cast ye the unprofitable servant into outer darkness: there shall be weeping and gnashing of teeth."

Father wants us to prosper. In our prosperity we show forth His glory in the earth. He does not want His children in lack and He has given us enough that we can use the gifts that are inside of us to advance the Kingdom of God and to advance ourselves personally. Use the tools and be Blessed! Patty and Andy learned the hard way!

Food for Thought

1) If Christ were to come in the next five minutes   what would be your return on His investment in you?

2) No man knows the day nor the hour when the Son of Man shall come, are you ready to trust God and use your gifts to tell a dying world about Christ?

Talent= a power of mind or body considered as given to a person for use and improvement: so called from the parable in Matt. 25:14–30.

Gift= Something that is bestowed voluntarily and without compensation. Can you see the difference between these two words?

The Tithe/The Offering

(The tenth of all your substance/As the Lord Prospers You)

Malachi 3:8-10 "Will a man rob God? Yet you rob me. But you ask, 'How do we rob you?' In tithes and offerings. You are under a curse—the whole nation of you—because you are robbing me. Bring the whole tithe into the storehouse, that there may be food in my house. Test me in this," says the LORD Almighty, "and see if I will not throw open the floodgates of heaven and pour out so much blessing that you will not have room enough for it." (NIV)

Is there anything wrong with this scripture?
Why do we suppose people are not willing to comply with God's Word?

2 Corinthians 9:6-11" Remember this: Whoever sows sparingly will also reap sparingly, and whoever sows

generously will also reap generously.
Each man should give what he has
decided in his heart to give, not
reluctantly or under compulsion, for God
loves a cheerful giver. And God is able
to make all grace abound to you, so that
in all things at all times, having all that
you need, you will abound in every good
work. As it is written: 'He has scattered
abroad his gifts to the poor; his
righteousness endures forever.' Now he
who supplies seed to the sower and
bread for food will also supply and
increase your store of seed and will
enlarge the harvest of your
righteousness. You will be made rich in
every way so that you can be generous
on every occasion, and through us your
generosity will result in thanksgiving to
God." (NIV)

New Testament Tithes are for those
who want to stretch their faith to enlarge
their territory!

The Prophetic Application

Apply the following principles to an everyday situation.

A prophet tells you that God said to write a book, CD. Movie what will you do?

God says to invest in property and make it a house for teen girls what would you do?

God has given you an inheritance and people around you are in need, how will you respond?

God says to open your house to teach others how to pray what is your response?

God says to go to a church and help them with your time, talent, and treasure. What do you do?

When God Speaks do you listen?

Prophesy to someone in your area.

Questions

1. What was the main characters' problem?

2. What was missing from the equation?

3. What scripture would you have used to encourage the main characters   ?

4. How will you now use this information to better serve Christ?

5. Well done thy _____ and_____
_____ enter _____ the ___ ___
_____

Why? Give examples

6. What happened to the servant with the one talent?

Why?
Share Your Lesson with family, friends and neighbors and the Lord will bless you for sowing seeds for the Kingdom

Lesson 4:

The Harvest
The Delegation of Power

Matthew 13:35-38 "And Jesus went about all the cities and villages, teaching in their synagogues, and preaching the gospel of the kingdom, and healing every sickness and every disease among the people. But when he saw the multitudes, he was moved with compassion on them, because they fainted, and were scattered abroad, as sheep having no shepherd. Then saith he unto his disciples, The harvest truly is plenteous, but the labourers are few; Pray ye therefore the Lord of the harvest, that he will send forth labourers into his harvest."

The nondenominational church at large has many problems with Evangelism in recent times. Many of the saints are unwilling to share their faith with others and there are so many that are "unchurched" who are waiting outside of the walls for someone to come out and tell them that Jesus lives.

My story is one that some may have experienced. It was 1981 and I had just experienced the death of my baby Vikki Donée. Vikki was the only child that I had out of five children that was born to the day that the doctors said so what happened to he afterward seemed so odd to me. Here we have a full term baby and she gets sick and ends up dying 3 and one half weeks into her life. What a time of sorrow. I felt as if I was going to die as well.

The Lord used my mother and my aunts to encourage me through this ordeal and they called upon the name of Jesus to help me. I did not know Him like I know Him now. To make a really long story short, time passes and I am going into a deep depression and I don't even know it. I have the windows closed, the blinds drawn and I am not receiving company or phone calls. My two older children were very young so they could not tell what was happening and my husband did not know what was happening.

I was so into my music that nothing and no one else mattered, I was lost! My Aunt El was an Evangelist at that time and she had heard what was going on with me. She came out of the four walls of her church and prayed on my porch for three Sundays straight until I opened the door and let her in.

I did not know I was angry with God, I did not know that I needed a shepherd to lead me, to comfort me. I only knew that if God allowed my baby to die then I must really be a bad person and so I needed someone like Aunt El to come and rescue me. If Aunt El had not come that day I don't know where I would be right now! She came and labored for the Lord and her labor was not in vain.

I thank God for her and those like her who are willing to go out into the harvest to do what Christ would do if He were here. Christ's mission on earth was to bring the lost to God. Our mission is to bring the Lost to the Cross to meet our Boss, Jesus Christ our Lord and Savior!

Matthew 13:35-38 "And Jesus went about all the cities and villages, teaching in their synagogues, and preaching the gospel of the kingdom, and healing every sickness and every disease among the people."

This is the job of the children of God. The great commission let's us know that we should go out into the world and baptize them in the name of the Father, Son and the Holy Ghost and teach and train them about the Gospel of Jesus Christ. We have power and authority to heal the sick, cast out devils and tread upon serpents. This is our inheritance!

"But when he saw the multitudes, he was moved with compassion on them, because they fainted, and were scattered abroad, as sheep having no shepherd."

More compassion is needed from the saints of God. There are too many who have now received Christ and are unwilling to let someone else know that He lives. The Bible says he who wins souls is wise. Many have fallen by the wayside and our strength in Christ will encourage them to stand up and get back in the race.

"Then saith he unto his disciples, The harvest truly is plenteous, but the labourers are few;"

Jesus is waiting for someone to pick up the mantle and continue the work. Labor to birth ministry, labor to bring souls to Christ, labor to open doors that are shut in the lives of the children of God. Spiritual Fathers and Mothers are needed to care for the many babies that have been left in the fields unattended.

"Pray ye therefore the Lord of the harvest, that he will send forth labourers into his harvest."

Father is looking for the true men and women of God to come forth and work in the harvest to advance the Kingdom of God.

There is a delegation of power and authority that has been released to the true men and women of God. Accept the call to Evangelize the nations. Start in your home, (Jerusalem) then in your community (Judea), then in your state (Samaria) and then in the uttermost parts of the world.

Food for Thought

1) If Christ were to come in the next five minutes   would you be able to give Him a list of souls you brought to Him?

2) No man knows the day nor the hour when the Son of Man shall come, are you ready to fulfill the great commission and bring the word of God to a dying world?

Harvest = the season when ripened crops are gathered.
Reap = to gather or take (a crop, harvest, etc.)To cut (wheat, rye, etc.) with a sickle or other implement or a machine, as in harvest.

In this case we are speaking of souls to be brought into the Kingdom!

Can you see the difference between these two words?

The Tithe/The Offering

(The tenth of all your substance/As the Lord Prospers You)

Malachi 3:8-10 "Will a man rob God? Yet you rob me. But you ask, 'How do we rob you?' In tithes and offerings. You are under a curse—the whole nation of you—because you are robbing me. Bring the whole tithe into the storehouse, that there may be food in my house. Test me in this," says the LORD Almighty, "and see if I will not throw open the floodgates of heaven and pour out so much blessing that you will not have room enough for it." (NIV)

Is there anything wrong with this scripture?
Why do we suppose people are not willing to comply with God's Word?

2 Corinthians 9:6-11" Remember this: Whoever sows sparingly will also reap sparingly, and whoever sows generously will also reap generously. Each man should give what he has decided in his heart to give, not

reluctantly or under compulsion, for God loves a cheerful giver. And God is able to make all grace abound to you, so that in all things at all times, having all that you need, you will abound in every good work. As it is written: 'He has scattered abroad his gifts to the poor; his righteousness endures forever.' Now he who supplies seed to the sower and bread for food will also supply and increase your store of seed and will enlarge the harvest of your righteousness. You will be made rich in every way so that you can be generous on every occasion, and through us your generosity will result in thanksgiving to God." (NIV)

New Testament Tithes are for those who want to stretch their faith to enlarge their territory!

The Prophetic Application

Apply the following principles to an everyday situation.

If the Pastor asks you to go out to evangelize what is your response?

How is your relationship with your neighbors?

Do they know about your church?

How do they view you? Are they aware that you are a Christian?Do you share your Faith with others?

Try taking tracts with you and word on the go tapes to sow into the lives of those you meet.

Are you aware that there is a crown waiting and for every soul you bring to God, he adds a jewel to your crown?

Start sharing your faith today!
Prophesy to someone in your area!

Questions

1. What was the main characters' problem?

2. What was missing from the equation?

3. What scripture would you have used to encourage the main characters   ?

4. How will you now use this information to better serve Christ?

5. The _____ _____ But the

_____

_____ are few.

Why? Give examples

6. What will happen if everyone helped to save just one soul per day?

Share Your Lesson with family, friends and neighbors and the Lord will bless you for sowing seeds for the Kingdom!

Lesson 5:

In Search of the Kingdom

Matthew 6:19-33 "Lay not up for yourselves treasures upon earth, where moth and rust doth corrupt, and where thieves break through and steal: But lay up for yourselves treasures in heaven, where neither moth nor rust doth corrupt, and where thieves do not break through nor steal: For where your treasure is, there will your heart be also. The light of the body is the eye: if therefore thine eye be single, thy whole body shall be full of light. But if thine eye be evil, thy whole body shall be full of darkness. If therefore the light that is in thee be darkness, how great is that darkness! No man can serve two masters: for either he will hate the one, and love the other; or else he will hold to the one, and despise the other. Ye cannot serve God and mammon. Therefore I say unto you, Take no thought for your life, what ye shall eat, or what ye shall drink; nor yet for your body, what ye shall put on. Is not the life more than meat, and the body than raiment? Behold the fowls of the air: for they sow not, neither do they reap, nor gather into barns; yet your heavenly Father feedeth them. Are ye not much better than they? Which of you by taking thought can add one cubit unto his stature? And why take ye thought for raiment? Consider the lilies of the field, how they grow; they toil not, neither do they spin: And yet I say unto you, That even Solomon in all his glory was not arrayed like one of these. Wherefore, if God so clothe the grass of the field, which to day is, and to morrow is cast into the oven, shall he not much more clothe you, O ye of little faith? Therefore take no thought, saying, What shall we eat? or, What shall we drink? or, Wherewithal shall we be clothed? (For after all these things do the Gentiles seek:) for your heavenly Father knoweth that ye have need of all these things. But seek ye first the kingdom of God, and his righteousness; and all these things shall be added unto you."

I often think about the commercial that says "First things first, obey your thirst".

Our thirst has to be for Christ to rule in reign in us on a daily basis. Over the years I have had numerous opportunities to speak with Pastors, lay people and sinners just to get an idea of what position the Lord holds in their everyday life. Much to my amazement for many, He was not first.

I have found that jobs, children, husbands, school, money, computer games, church and ministry held a higher position in their lives than their actual relationship with Him. Some found themselves wrapped up in the creation, rather than the Creator and this caused them to be out of alignment with the word of God.

The Bible says to seek first the Kingdom of God and its righteousness, and we know now that the first place to look is inside of ourselves because that is where the Kingdom lies.

We are also the righteousness of God In Christ Jesus and God's Kingdom is in us. We have the power to pull up power from inside to deliver us from any situation. Everything we need is already on the inside of us. We have power to multiply our gifts, increase our worth and enlarge our territories if we seek that which is inside of us. The Holy Spirit is inside of us waiting to be enquired of. Just Ask!

Matthew 6:19-33 "Lay not up for yourselves treasures upon earth, where moth and rust doth corrupt, and where thieves break through and steal:
Do not worship temporal things which can decay, or rot or be stolen. But lay up for yourselves treasures in heaven, where neither moth nor rust doth corrupt, and where thieves do not break through nor steal: But sow to the Spirit and we will inherit treasures in heaven that nothing can decay it, and no one can steal it. It is our inheritance as

children of God. For where your treasure is, there will your heart be also.

We can always tell what is really important to a person by their reaction when they have to give. If they are asked to sow money and they have a problem with it, their heart is deceived by money. Freely God has given us freely we should give back to Him. Therefore I say unto you, Take no thought for your life, what ye shall eat, or what ye shall drink; nor yet for your body, what ye shall put on. Is not the life more than meat, and the body than raiment?"

Stop worrying! I have a few friends who are so worried about what they will have when they get old. Our Father told us He will supply all of our needs according to His riches in Glory which is in Christ Jesus. We must believe that.

"Behold the fowls of the air: for they sow not, neither do they reap, nor gather into barns; yet your heavenly Father feedeth them. Are ye not much better than they? Never has He forsaken the righteous. Why do we doubt Him now? Which of you by taking thought can add one cubit unto his stature?"

We cannot change our height. He already knows everything, we need to trust Him!

"And why take ye thought for raiment? Consider the lilies of the field, how they grow; they toil not, neither do they spin:"

Clothing is not even a worry; we have always had more than enough. If He will take care of lilies in the field are we not more than those?

"And yet I say unto you, that even Solomon in all his glory was not arrayed like one of these."

Read about Solomon He was dressed to impress and yet He could not make himself look better than the flowers in the field, and all he had belonged to God. Solomon Loved God!

"Wherefore, if God so clothe the grass of the field, which to day is, and to morrow is cast into the oven, shall he not much more clothe you, O ye of little faith?"

Why do we keep God in a Box? He has clothed the grass, He can clothe us!

"Therefore take no thought, saying, What shall we eat? or, What shall we drink? or, Wherewithal shall we be clothed?"

Don't Worry! Worry profits you nothing since His will is what will be done no matter what. Worry causes dis-ease, dis-ease causes spiritual and physical death.

"(For after all these things do the Gentiles seek:) for your heavenly Father knoweth that ye have need of all these things."

Gentiles in our day are those who have not met Jesus as Lord and King.

Many that have not met Him are stuck on what the material world can give them, the latest fad, what would make someone else jealous, or how they can get one up on someone. The lust of the eyes, pride of life, and the lust of the flesh is their concern. Father is saying I know what you have need of Trust me to be your Jehovah Jira and provide for you all that you need.

"But seek ye first the kingdom of God, and his righteousness; and all these things shall be added unto you".
First things first. Seek me first and everything else will come after that. The Bible says He is a rewarder of those who diligently seek Him (**Heb 11:6**)

Jer. 29:13 "And ye shall seek me, and find me, when ye shall search for me with all your heart."

Search for Him, Chase after God and never lose His presence in your life. In the Ten Commandments we find God saying to Moses and the Hebrew Children that He is a jealous God and that there shall be no other gods before Him.

This is so obvious that the Lord knew that we would put gods before Him like our money gods, husband gods, children gods, cars, house, jobs, friends, TV, movies, ministries, and whatever else can consume our time so that we will be out of His presence. When out of the presence of the Lord we cannot hear or get information to be successful. (**Joshua 1:8**) This book of the law shall not depart out of thy mouth; but thou shalt meditate therein day and night, that thou mayest observe to do according to all that is written therein: for then thou shalt make thy way prosperous, and then thou shalt have good success. Seek God and receive the Promise!

Food for Thought

1) If Christ were to come in the next five minutes would you drop all that you were doing to give Him Glory? Would you discern that it was HIM?

2) No man knows the day nor the hour when the Son of Man shall come, are you ready to be a God Chaser? One who will chase God to receive His Kingdom?

Seek= to go in search or quest of: to seek the truth. To try to find or discover by searching or questioning: to seek the solution to a problem.

Search = to look at or beneath the superficial aspects of to discover a motive, reaction, feeling, basic truth, etc. to look at or examine carefully in order to find something concealed

Can you see the difference between these two words?

The Tithe/The Offering

(The tenth of all your substance/As the Lord Prospers You)
Malachi 3:8-10 "Will a man rob God? Yet you rob me. But you ask, 'How do we rob you?' In tithes and offerings. You are under a curse—the whole nation of you—because you are robbing me. Bring the whole tithe into the storehouse, that there may be food in my house. Test me in this," says the LORD Almighty, "and see if I will not throw open the floodgates of heaven and pour out so much blessing that you will not have room enough for it." (NIV)

Is there anything wrong with this scripture?
Why do we suppose people are not willing to comply with God's Word?

2 Corinthians 9:6-11" Remember this: Whoever sows sparingly will also reap sparingly, and whoever sows generously will also reap generously. Each man should give what he has decided in his heart to give, not

reluctantly or under compulsion, for God loves a cheerful giver. And God is able to make all grace abound to you, so that in all things at all times, having all that you need, you will abound in every good work. As it is written: 'He has scattered abroad his gifts to the poor; his righteousness endures forever.' Now he who supplies seed to the sower and bread for food will also supply and increase your store of seed and will enlarge the harvest of your righteousness. You will be made rich in every way so that you can be generous on every occasion, and through us your generosity will result in thanksgiving to God." (NIV)

New Testament Tithes are for those who want to stretch their faith to enlarge their territory!

The Prophetic Application

Apply the following principles to an everyday situation.

There is a sale at Macy's on Sunday morning and I am scheduled to do intercessory prayer, whatever will I Do?

My friend is in the hospital and is in need of prayer but I wanted to see the new movie that came out what will I do?

The church is need of extra finances and I am just dying to upgrade my Blackberry! What will I do?

I need to write this book but that computer game seems to be so exciting what will I do?

This guy/girl is so cute but He/she is not a believer and does not want to go to church what will I do?

I have made a promise to be somewhere to help with a project but I really want to go out and eat with my friends what will I do?

I have been called by God to do a ministry
What will I do?

Prophesy to someone in your area.

Questions

1. What was the main characters' problem?

2. What was missing from the equation?

3. What scripture would you have used to encourage the main characters   ?

4. How will you now use this information to better serve Christ?

5. And ye _____ _____ Me and find _____ when you _____ _____for Me _____ _____ your _____

6. How do we seek God? Give examples

7. What happens when you seek first the Kingdom of God?

Share Your Lesson with family, friends and neighbors and the Lord will bless you for sowing seeds for the Kingdom!

Christ Is The Only Answer!

The Bible says in **Romans 10:9-10** "That if you confess with your mouth, "Jesus is Lord," and believe in your heart that God raised him from the dead, you will be saved." For it is with your heart that you believe and are justified, and it is with your mouth that you confess and are saved. (NIV)

If you have said these simple words the Lord has heard your cry and has already delivered you. Please find yourself a Bible believing church and plant yourself there. Be trained and equipped for Kingdom Building.

Grace and Peace,

Apostle G. Marie Carroll

For Information about this book or any
other ministry tool from Kingdom
Builders please contact us.

Kingdom Builders International
Movement For Christ Inc
610 Woodfield Road
West Hempstead NY 11552
516 833-5235
Bishop Kenneth Carroll
Apostle G. Marie Carroll
Kingdombuilders669@yahoo.com
www.gmarieworldwide.com
www.myspace.com/apostlegmarie
www.facebook.com/kingdombuilders

Ministry Tools
The power of The Five-Fold
(For the perfecting of the Saints)
If there is no Power There is no Prayer!!
Why Me? So it doesn't have to be you
(Blaze)
A Good Thins
(For the Manifestation of Your mate)
(Blaze)

Tapes and Word to Go also available

55273938R00050

Made in the USA
Charleston, SC
25 April 2016